MiXed-UP PUPS

BY ED MASESSA

SCHOLASTIC INC.

PHOTO CREDITS

Front cover center: Kimball Stock; front cover left: Lancaster Puppies; front cover right: Exactostock/SuperStock; back cover: Kimball Stock; 3 background: Kimball Stock; 3 bottom: RTimages/Alamy; 3 left: ibid; 3 center: Kimball Stock; 3 right: ibid; 4 top left: Life on White/Alamy; 4 top right: Utekhina Anna/Shutterstock; 4 bottom: Lancaster Puppies; 7 top left: cynoclub/Shutterstock; 7 top right: Jagodka/Shutterstock; 7 bottom: Ocean/Corbis; 8 top left: Nick Wright/Media Bakery; 8 top right: Andrew Grant/Corbis; 8 bottom: RTimages/Alamy; 11 top left: Eric Isselée/Shutterstock; 11 top right: Yco/Shutterstock; 11 bottom: Lancaster Puppies; 12 top left: Stockbroker xtra/age fotostock; 12 top right: Jagodka/Shutterstock; 12 bottom: Exactostock/SuperStock; 15 top left: Hannamariah/Shutterstock; 15 top right: iStockphoto; 15 bottom: Lancaster Puppies; 16 top left: Fly_dragonfly/Shutterstock; 16 top right: Degtyaryov Andrey Leonidovich/Shutterstock; 16 bottom: Kimball Stock; 19 top left: mariait/Shutterstock; 19 top right: Life on White/Alamy; 19 bottom: Kimball Stock; 20 top left: Lars Christensen/Shutterstock; 20 top right: Andrii Muzyka/Shutterstock; 20 bottom: Kimball Stock; 23 top left: Erik Lam/Alamy; 23 top right: Nikolai Tsvetkov/Shutterstock; 23 bottom: Lancaster Puppies; 24 top left: Eric Isselée/Shutterstock; 24 top right: GorillaAttack/Shutterstock; 24 bottom: Lancaster Puppies; 27 top left: Dorottya Mathe/Shutterstock; 27 top right: Eric Isselée/Shutterstock; 27 bottom: imagebroker.net/SuperStock; 28 top left: Ruthblack/Dreamstime; 28 top right: Allison Michael Orenstein/Getty Images; 28 bottom: Kimball Stock; 31 top left: Lilia Beck/Shutterstock; 31 top right: Kimball Stock

ISBN 978-0-545-53244-0

12 11 10 9 8 7 6 5 4 3 2 1   13 14 15 16 17 18/0

Printed in the U.S.A   40
First printing, January 2013
Designed by Carla Alpert

HYBRID

Hybrid is a good word to know. When a car is a hybrid, it can run on two kinds of fuel. But when a dog is a hybrid, it is a cross between two different *breeds* of dogs. Some people call them designer dogs. You can call them mixed-up pups!

CHIHUAHUA

YORKSHIRE TERRIER

CHORKIE

CHORKIE

A **CHORKIE** is a cross between a Chihuahua and a Yorkshire Terrier. Chihuahuas are smart and Yorkies are cute. When you mix them up you get a very popular puppy! A Chorkie puppy is so small it can fit in the palm of your hand. Some have short hair, some have long hair, but they all love to play.

ANYTHING IS POSSIBLE! Your dad has brown eyes and your mom's are blue. So how did you get green eyes? Your mom and dad have black hair, but yours is light brown. The same thing happens when you mix up two breeds of dogs.

LABRADOODLE

A **LABRADOODLE** is a cross between a Labrador Retriever and a Poodle. The Lab is a wonderful, friendly, family dog, and the Poodle has the kind of fur that doesn't bother most people who have *allergies*. Mixed together, they make the perfect pet! The size of the Labradoodle depends mainly on the size of the Poodle.

Ah . . . AH . . . *ACHOO!* Some people are allergic to dogs, and usually it's because of the dander — or dead skin — that comes off when a dog *sheds* its fur. Wouldn't a danderless dog be just dandy? Poodle fur produces less dander and is called *hypoallergenic*.

LABRADOR RETRIEVER

POODLE

LABRADOODLE

COCKER SPANIEL

POODLE

COCKAPOO

COCKAPOO

A **COCKAPOO** is a cross between a Cocker Spaniel and a Poodle. Cockapoos are smart and happy and love to spend time with their human friends. A Poodle has a curly *coat*, and the Cocker Spaniel has a flat coat — so a Cockapoo could have either!

☆ PUGGLE ☆

A **PUGGLE** is a cross between a Pug and a Beagle. Both Pugs and Beagles are cheerful and friendly with children, but they both can be very *stubborn*. A Pug has a short curly tail, and a Beagle has a long straight one. What will your Puggle's tail look like?

FUN FACT!
A baby echidna is also called a puggle!

PUG

BEAGLE

PUGGLE

SCHNAUZER

POODLE

SCHNOODLE

SCHNOODLE

A **SCHNOODLE** is a cross between a Schnauzer and a Poodle. Both the Schnauzer and the Poodle come in sizes from very large to very small. But the *Miniature* Schnoodle is the most common size. It is smart and playful. If you like to run, jump, play catch, or have a good tug-of-war, the Schnoodle is the dog for you!

OODLES OF POODLES! The Poodle has a non-shedding coat, which many people like. When a Poodle is crossed with another dog breed, you usually get a dog that doesn't shed . . . which means less vacuuming!

DOUBLE DOODLE

A **DOUBLE DOODLE** is a cross between a Goldendoodle and a Labradoodle. Because it's a cross between three dog breeds, anything is possible. But one thing you can count on — it will be a friendly, kind, double-doodle dandy of a dog! I double-dog dare you to say *Double Doodle* three times fast.

GOLDEN DOODLE

LABRADOODLE

DOUBLE DOODLE

JACK RUSSELL TERRIER

PEMBROKE WELSH CORGI

COJACK

A **COJACK** is a cross between a Jack Russell Terrier and a Pembroke Welsh Corgi and, like both of its parents, it is full of energy and needs a lot of exercise. The Corgi is used for *herding* cows, and the Jack is a spunky jumper. The Cojack will definitely keep you busy!

SNORKIE

A **SNORKIE** is a cross between a Miniature Schnauzer and a Yorkshire Terrier. If you were a teacher, this would be your best student! It is eager to learn new tricks and happy to perform them. But it's very small, so don't get too rough.

MINIATURE SCHNAUZER

YORKSHIRE TERRIER

SNORKIE

CAIRN TERRIER

MINIATURE SCHNAUZER

CARNAUZER

A **CARNAUZER** is a cross between a Cairn Terrier and a Miniature Schnauzer. This peppy puppy will chase a ball for as long as you feel like throwing one. It has the short legs of the Cairn and the square-shaped head and *sturdy* body of the Schnauzer. Kids can count on the Carnauzer to be their lifelong friend.

CHIWEENIE

A **CHIWEENIE** is a cross between a Chihuahua and a Dachshund. The Chiweenie could have long, floppy ears or perky, pointed ones. It's named a Chiweenie because it has a long, round body like a hot dog, which is sometimes called a wiener dog! It constantly wags its tail because it's always happy to see you.

CHIHUAHUA

DACHSHUND

CHIWEENIE

JACK RUSSELL TERRIER

PUG

JUG

JUG

A **JUG** is a cross between a Jack Russell Terrier and a Pug. This little guy is really mixed up! It usually has the short, round face of the Pug, the lean body of the Jack, and the curly tail of the Pug. The Pug and the Jack are very smart dogs, so the Jug just might be able to help you with your homework!

WHATCHAMACALLIT! Your mom's family name is Smith. Your dad's family name is Jones. You might be Emily Smith-Jones or Jimmy Jones-Smith, but definitely not Emily Smones or Jimmy Jith. Yet a Pug and a Jack is a Jug! Huh?

HAVAMALT

A HAVAMALT is a cross between a Havanese and a Maltese. This is a big ball of love wrapped inside a fluffy little dog. And its double coat is great for people who have allergies! Brush your Havamalt often to keep it looking pretty and give it a special treat for being your best friend.

HAVANESE

MALTESE

HAVAMALT

LHASA APSO

MINIATURE POODLE

LHASA-POO

28

LHASA-POO

A **LHASA-POO** is a cross between a Lhasa Apso and a Miniature Poodle. This little sweetheart looks more like a stuffed animal than a real dog. And look at those eyes! Its coat is soft and silky — just right for cuddling. But it is also timid, or shy, so be extra gentle when you pet it.

BEABULL

A **BEABULL** is a cross between a Beagle and a Bulldog. Most of the time, the Beabull likes to lie around the house. But give it a chew toy and there will not be much left of it when it's done. It also sheds a lot of hair, so be nice and help with the cleaning.

SPOOKY FACT! A Bogle is a cross between a Beagle and a Boxer, but it is also another word for a ghost! If you owned one, you could name it Casper!

BEAGLE

BULLDOG

BEABULL

GLOSSARY

ALLERGY – A reaction to a substance which causes you to sneeze, develop a rash, or have another unpleasant response.

BREED – A particular type of plant or animal.

COAT – An animal's covering of hair or fur.

HERDING – Moving people or animals together in a group.

HYBRID – Something that is made by combining two or more things.

HYPOALLERGENIC – Unlikely to cause an allergic reaction.

MINIATURE – Much smaller than usual.

SHED – To lose, to get rid of, or to let something fall.

STUBBORN – Not willing to give in or change; set on having your own way.

STURDY – Strong and solidly made or built.